BIRDHOUSES

Renée Schwarz

KIDS CAN PRESS

To Alex, Sophie and Pippa, my baby birds
And to Dédé, my birdman.

Kids Can Press acknowledges the financial support of the Government of Ontario, through the Ontario Media Development Corporation's Ontario Book Initiative, and the Government of Canada, through the BPIDP, for our publishing activity.

Published in Canada by
Kids Can Press Ltd.
29 Birch Avenue
Toronto, ON M4V 1E2

Published in the U.S. by
Kids Can Press Ltd.
2250 Military Road
Tonawanda, NY 14150

www.kidscanpress.com

Edited by Stacey Roderick
Designed by Karen Powers
Cover photography by Frank Baldassarra

Printed and bound in China

The hardcover edition of this book is smyth sewn casebound.
The paperback edition of this book is limp sewn with a drawn-on cover.

CM 05 0 9 8 7 6 5 4 3 2 1
CM PA 05 0 9 8 7 6 5 4 3 2 1

National Library of Canada Cataloguing in Publication Data

Schwarz, Renée
        Birdhouses / Renée Schwarz.

(Kids can do it)
ISBN 1-55337-549-1 (bound).   ISBN 1-55337-550-5 (pbk.)

1. Birdhouses — Design and construction — Juvenile literature. I. Title. II. Series.

QL676.5.S35 2005   j690'.8927   C2004-901930-9

Kids Can Press is a ᴸᴼᴿᵁˢ™ Entertainment company

Contents

More birdhouse information on inside back cover

Introduction

Building birdhouses is a great way to get chickadees, bluebirds, swallows, wrens and many other kinds of birds to nest in your backyard. And with fewer old trees around for birds to nest in, building birdhouses is not only fun, it's important.

The simple woodworking skills you need to make these birdhouses are easy to learn, even if you've never used a hammer or saw. And don't worry if your first houses are a bit lopsided — the birds won't mind!

Most of the houses can be made in an afternoon and will last for years. Be creative and change the designs or sizes, but always make them safe for the birds. Check the chart on the inside back cover of the book for help adapting the projects to different birds.

Building birdhouses is fun, but the best part is when birds nest in them. The sky's the limit!

MATERIALS AND TOOLS

The materials and tools you will need are sold in hardware stores. Also look around your home for extra wooden boards, nails and screws, etc., but always ask first if you can use things.

You will need pencils and rulers to mark and measure materials. Remember to always measure twice so you only have to cut once!

Wood is sold in standard thicknesses and widths that are measured in inches, even though their actual sizes are a bit smaller. For example, if you measured a 1 x 6 board, its real size would be $3/4$ in. x $5\frac{1}{2}$ in. Common boards are 1 x 2s, 1 x 4s, 1 x 5s, 1 x 6s, 1 x 8s and 1 x 10s. For the projects in this book, buy boards that are the standard thicknesses and widths listed, but cut the exact lengths.

Most of the wood used is 1 inch-thick pine because it is strong, cuts easily and protects the birds from the weather. Exterior grade plywood can be used, too, but nails and screws do not hold as well in the cut edges. Do not use treated wood.

▷ **Other wood you will use**

scoop molding

half-round molding

pine slats

dowels

wooden beads and knobs

precut wooden decorations

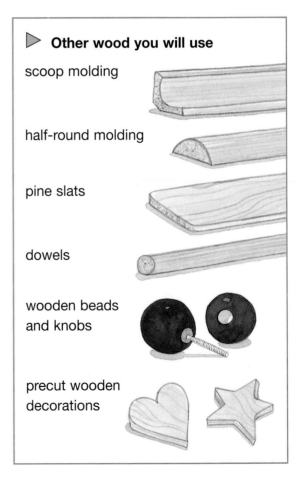

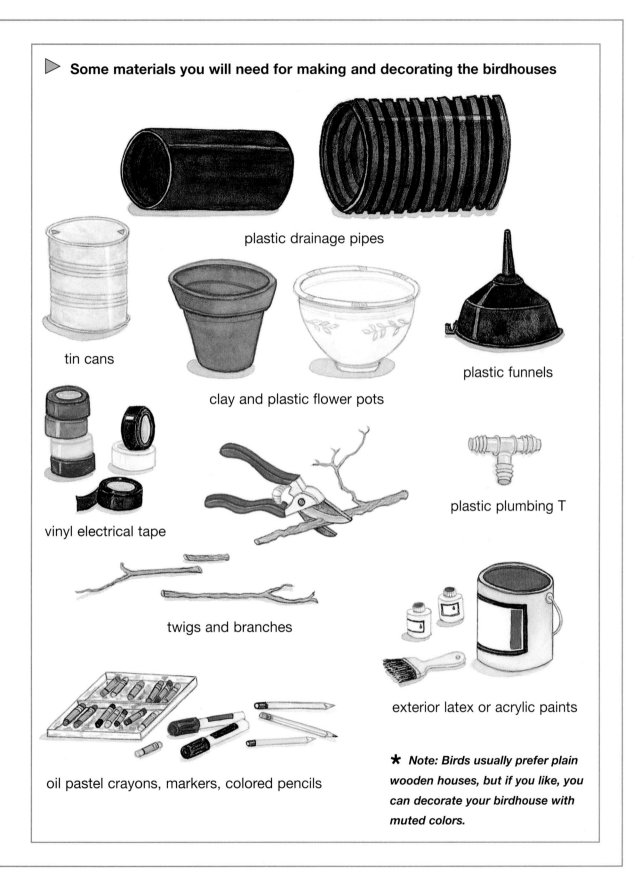

▷ Some materials you will need for making and decorating the birdhouses

plastic drainage pipes

tin cans

clay and plastic flower pots

plastic funnels

vinyl electrical tape

plastic plumbing T

twigs and branches

exterior latex or acrylic paints

oil pastel crayons, markers, colored pencils

* Note: Birds usually prefer plain wooden houses, but if you like, you can decorate your birdhouse with muted colors.

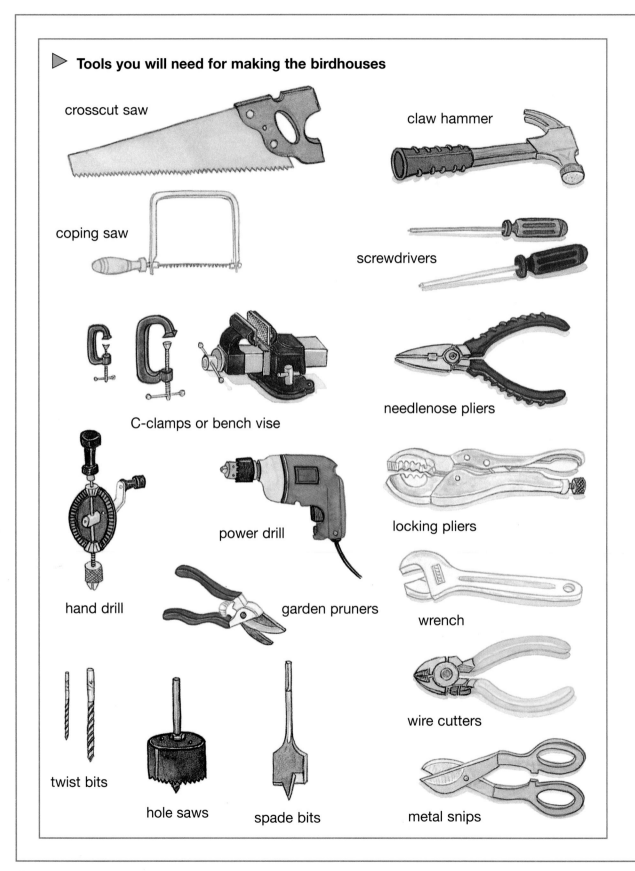

▷ Tools you will need for making the birdhouses

crosscut saw

claw hammer

coping saw

screwdrivers

C-clamps or bench vise

needlenose pliers

hand drill

power drill

locking pliers

garden pruners

wrench

wire cutters

twist bits

hole saws

spade bits

metal snips

▷ **For assembling the birdhouses, you will need**

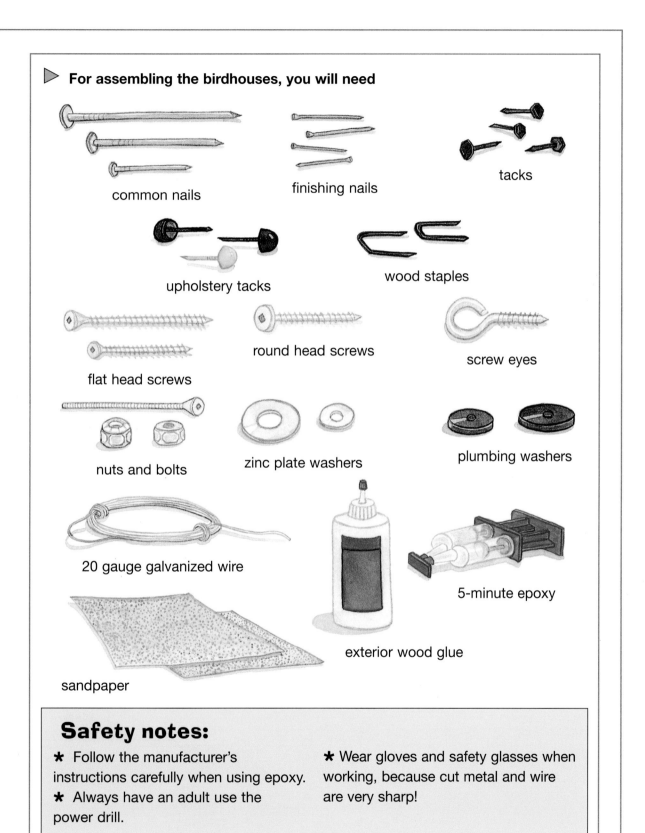

common nails

finishing nails

tacks

upholstery tacks

wood staples

flat head screws

round head screws

screw eyes

nuts and bolts

zinc plate washers

plumbing washers

20 gauge galvanized wire

exterior wood glue

5-minute epoxy

sandpaper

Safety notes:

✳ Follow the manufacturer's instructions carefully when using epoxy.
✳ Always have an adult use the power drill.

✳ Wear gloves and safety glasses when working, because cut metal and wire are very sharp!

Woodworking techniques

Before starting any of the projects in the book, read this section and ask an adult to show you how to use the tools.

Safety

Hand tools are safe when used carefully and properly. Always protect yourself by wearing safety glasses and work gloves, especially when sawing, drilling or cutting. Never force tools, because they can slip and hurt you. Take your time and, if something is too difficult, ask an adult for help. And always ask an adult to use the power drill when it is needed.

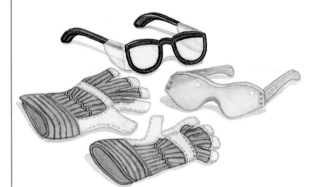

Work surface

It is best to use a worktable or workbench. A large wooden board can also be used as your work surface. Keep your work area clean. Sweep up sawdust — it can be slippery!

Clamping

You can use either a C-clamp or a bench vise to hold the wood. It is important to clamp wood to your work surface so it does not move when you are sawing or drilling. The illustrations will show you how to place the wood. Small pieces like branches are difficult to hold in a clamp or vise — you may want to ask a helper to hold them in place.

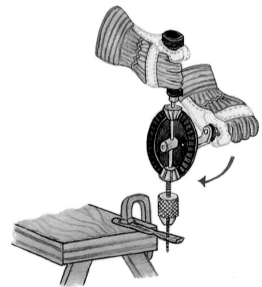

Sawing

Wearing work gloves and safety glasses, clamp the wood to your work surface as shown. Try not to saw, drill or nail through knots in the wood.

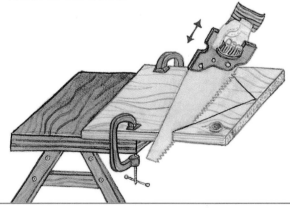

To saw, first pull the saw back slowly a few times to make a notch for the blade. Continue with full strokes. Just let the saw slide — if you push too hard, it will stick or buckle. Try to keep the saw at a 45° angle. Near the end of the cut, hold the part that is not clamped so it does not break off.

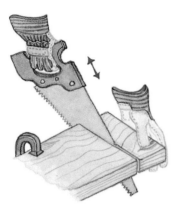

Coping saws cut round shapes and decorative pieces. Draw the shape onto the wood, near the edge. Clamp the board to your work surface and cut the shape out. It is usually easier to make a few cuts that start at different points and meet than to saw the whole piece with one cut. Use sandpaper to smooth rough edges.

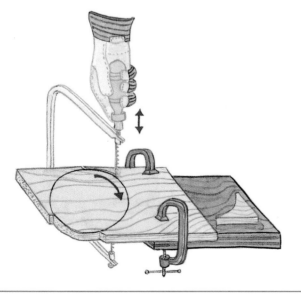

Drilling

Always wear safety glasses and work gloves, and clamp the piece down securely so it does not spin. Have the part of the board being drilled extend past your work surface. Or place a scrap piece of wood underneath first so you don't drill into the table.

Drill bits fit into the chuck, or bit holder, and are held in place by tightening the outer ring of the chuck clockwise (to the right). The size of the hole made depends on the size of the bit used.

Use a hand drill for drilling air, drainage and mounting holes and for drilling pilot holes before nailing or screwing.

Use a power drill with a hole saw or spade bit for drilling entrance holes. Mark the center of the hole and then ask an adult to drill it.

Nailing

Hold the nail in place between your thumb and finger as shown. Tap the head of the nail lightly with the hammer until it stands up in the wood. Remove your fingers and hammer a bit harder. When the nail is well in, hammer with hard strokes. If the nail bends, pull it out with the claw part of the hammer.

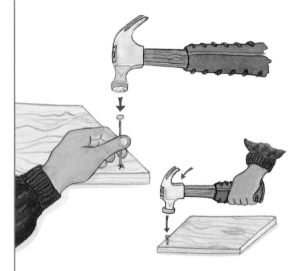

When nailing thin wood slats or branches, drill small pilot holes first so the wood doesn't split.

Nails should not poke through on the inside of your finished birdhouse! If they do, hammer them flat so there are no sharp points.

Screwing

Screws are stronger than nails but can be easily unscrewed and removed. Choose a screwdriver that fits the slot on the head of the screw. The screwdriver tip should fit tightly so that it does not slip out when turned. Drill small pilot holes first if the wood begins to split. Screws, screw eyes, nuts and bolts always turn clockwise (to the right) to tighten and counterclockwise (to the left) to loosen. Just remember: "lefty-loosey, righty-tighty."

Tips for mounting and care

Hang your birdhouses on fence posts, in trees or on buildings. Different birds like different spots. Check the chart at the back of the book to see what is best.

● If you have drilled mounting holes in the back of the birdhouse, attach it using screws or wire.

● For houses with no mounting holes, you can screw corner braces or angles to the back corners of the house for mounting it.

● Place the house where there is some shade during the day.

● If possible, face the entrance hole east: birds like the morning sun!

● Place the house where cats can't climb up or jump on it.

● Be sure to make floor drainage holes and air holes.

● Early in the spring, wear gloves to clean out the house by unscrewing the floor. Also check to see if anything needs to be fixed.

● If no birds choose your birdhouse after a year or two, try moving it to another spot.

Robin's delight

For robins, who prefer the open air.

You will need

- two pine boards: 1 x 8 x 15 cm (6 in.)
- thin branches or twigs • three 2 in. common nails
- about 40 1 in. common nails
- four 1 m (40 in.) lengths of 20 gauge galvanized wire
- small precut wooden hearts • red oil pastel crayon
- pencil and ruler • work gloves and safety glasses
- C-clamps, saw, hammer, hand drill with a 1/4 in. bit and a 1/16 in. bit, garden pruners, wire cutters

1 For the bottom, hammer the three 2 in. nails into one board about 1 cm (1/2 in.) from the edge of a short side, one in the middle and one near each end. The nails should just poke through the other side.

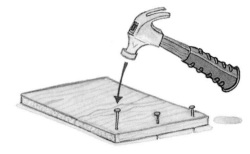

2 Place the two boards together, as shown, and nail them together.

3 Clamp the back board to your work surface. Mark two mounting holes 5 cm (2 in.) from the top. Hand drill 1/4 in. holes.

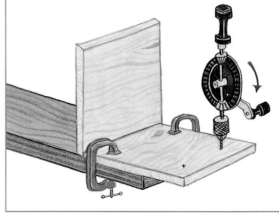

4 Use garden pruners to carefully cut the branches into seventeen 9 cm (3½ in.) lengths, three 23 cm (9 in.) lengths and fifteen to twenty 20 cm (8 in.) lengths.

i So the branches don't split when nailing, hand drill ¹/₁₆ in. holes about 1 cm (½ in.) from one end. Clamp the branches to your work surface or have someone hold them while you drill.

i For the fence, nail the 9 cm (3½ in.) posts about 2 cm (¾ in.) apart (five along the front and six along each side). Nail two 23 cm (9 in.) branches to the back board, as shown.

7 For the roof, nail the 20 cm (8 in.) branches to the top as tightly together as possible.

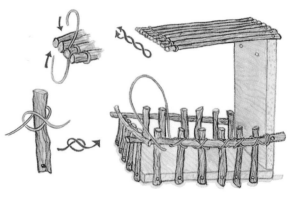

8 Using one strand of wire for each side, wind wire around the posts and crosspieces to hold them together. Also wire a 23 cm (9 in.) branch across the front. Wire the roof branches together near the front.

9 Color the wooden hearts and nail them on as decoration.

Moon shelf

For phoebes and other birds who like to sleep under the stars.

You will need

- pine boards: 1 x 6 x 25 cm (10 in.),
  1 x 8 x 14 cm (5½ in.), 1 x 8 x 15 cm (6 in.),
  1 x 8 x 13 cm (5¼ in.)
- two 22 cm (8¾ in.) lengths of ¾ in. half-round molding
- small precut wooden stars and moon
- ten 2 in. common nails • four ¾ in. finishing nails
- exterior wood glue and damp rag
- pencil, ruler, oil pastel crayons
- work gloves and safety glasses
- C-clamps, saw, hammer, hand drill with a ¼ in. bit, coping saw

1 For the back, hammer three 2 in. nails into the 25 cm (10 in.) board about 1 cm (½ in.) from the edge of a short side, one in the middle and one near each end. The nails should just poke through the other side.

2 Spread glue on one short edge of the 14 cm (5½ in.) board. Place the boards as shown and nail them together. Wipe off any extra glue.

3 Clamp the back board to your work surface. Mark two mounting holes about 1.5 cm (⅝ in.) from the top. Hand drill ¼ in. holes.

4 Hammer three 2 in. nails along the longer edge of the 15 cm (6 in.) board as in step 1.

Spread glue on one long edge of the 13 cm (5¼ in.) board. Nail the roof boards together as shown. Wipe off any extra glue.

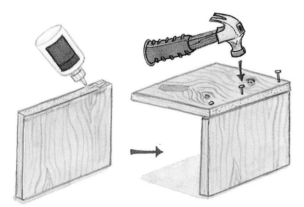

Nail the back board to the roof using the 2 in. nails. The peak of the roof should be higher than the back, as shown.

7 Place the molding against the front of the shelf, as shown. Mark the top edge of the roof on the flat side of the molding. Cut along the line with the coping saw.

8 Glue the molding in place, wiping off any excess glue. Hammer in the finishing nails, as shown.

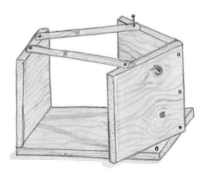

9 Color the stars and moon and glue them on as decorations.

Sunflower pot

A sunny birdhouse to rent to wrens.

You will need

- one glazed or varnished clay flowerpot, about 16 cm (6 ¼ in.) diameter
- pine boards: 1 x 8 x 17 cm (6 ¾ in.), 1 x 2 x 40 cm (16 in.), 1 x 2 x 5 cm (2 in.)
- seventeen ⅛ in. pine slats, 1 ¼ in. x 8 cm (3 in.)
- about forty ¾ in. finishing nails
- sixty to eighty black ¾ in. tacks
- one 2 in. bolt and locknut • one black plumbing washer
- four 1 ¼ in. screw eyes
- four 10 cm (4 in.) lengths and a 2 m (80 in.) length of 20 gauge galvanized wire
- yellow, light brown, black and green oil pastel crayons
- pencil, ruler, exterior wood glue and damp rag
- work gloves and safety glasses
- C-clamps, hammer, hand drill with a ⁵⁄₁₆ in. bit and a ¹⁄₁₆ in. bit, power drill and 1 ¼ in. hole saw, coping saw, screwdriver, locking pliers or wrench

1 Place the pot upside down on the 17 cm (6 ¾ in.) board. One side should stick out about 2 cm (¾ in.) past the edge of the board. Trace around the pot's edge with a pencil.

2 Remove the pot. Draw a circle about 1 cm (½ in.) outside the first circle, as shown.

3 Clamp the board to your work surface. Mark an X in the center, 11.5 cm (4 ½ in.) up from the straight edge. Ask an adult to drill a 1 ¼ in. entrance hole over the X using the power drill.

4 Hand drill three ⁵⁄₁₆ in. air holes on each side of the entrance hole, as shown.

5 Using the coping saw, cut out the circle along the outer line. Don't worry if the circle isn't perfect — its edges will be hidden.

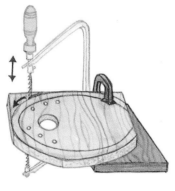

6 For each of the seventeen petals, draw a petal tip onto one end of a pine slat. Clamp the slat and cut the tip out with the coping saw.

7 Color the petals yellow and light brown roughly and smudge them lightly. Color the center of the flower (inside the circle) black. Color the 40 cm (16 in.) board green for the stem.

8 Dab some glue on the back of the petals, and nail them around the flower center using two finishing nails for each petal. If the wood splits, hand drill ¹⁄₁₆ in. pilot holes first.

9 Hammer tacks in the center of the flower to look like seeds.

10 Clamp the 40 cm (16 in.) board to your work surface. Mark and hand drill two ⁵⁄₁₆ in. holes, one 2.5 cm (1 in.) and another 11 cm (4¼ in.) from each end.

1 Clamp the 5 cm (2 in.) board to your work surface. Mark and hand drill a 5/16 in. hole in the center.

12 Slip the bolt through a hole on the 40 cm (16 in.) board, as shown. Next, slip on the pot, followed by the washer and then the 5 cm (2 in.) board.

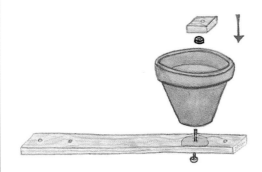

13 Grasping the locknut with the locking pliers or wrench, use the screwdriver to screw the nut onto the bolt. Tighten it gently so the pot doesn't crack.

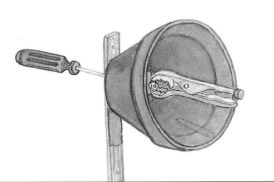

14 Place the pot upside down on the back of the flower, leaving a gap at the bottom for drainage. Mark four Xs, as shown. Remove the pot and screw in a screw eye at each X.

15 Slip a bent 10 cm (4 in.) length of wire through each screw eye. Twist once to hold.

16 Place the pot between the screw eyes. Wind the 2 m (80 in.) wire around the pot a few times, threading it through the screw eye wires. Twist the ends together, and then twist the screw eye wire ends to hold the pot tightly to the flower.

I love you bird box

Swallows need a little ladder inside so the baby birds can get out.

1 For the front, mark an X in the center of the 8 x 23 cm (9 in.) board, 17 cm (6 ¾ in.) from one shorter edge.

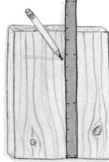

2 Clamp the board to your work surface, and ask an adult to drill a 1 ½ in. entrance hole over the X using the power drill.

3 To make a ladder for inside the house, saw four grooves below the hole, about 2 cm (¾ in.) apart, as shown.

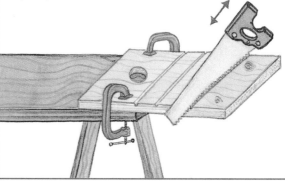

4 On the 54 cm (21½ in.) board, mark 30 cm (12 in.) on one edge and 23.5 cm (9¼ in.) on the other. Using a ruler, draw a line to join the marks. Clamp the board and saw along the line to make the two sides of the house.

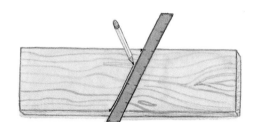

5 For each side, clamp and then hand drill three ¼ in. air holes, about 2.5 cm (1 in.) from the angled edge, as shown.

6 For the back, clamp the 40 cm (16 in.) board and mark four mounting holes about 2.5 cm (1 in.) in from the top and bottom corners. Hand drill ¼ in. holes.

7 Hammer six 2 in. nails into the front board, about 1 cm (½ in.) from each edge, one in the middle and one near each end. The nails should just poke through the other side.

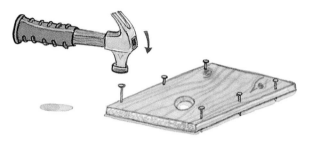

8 Place the front board about 1 cm (½ in.) below the top edges of the side boards, as shown. Nail the boards together.

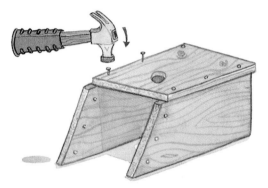

9 Place the back board about 5 cm (2 in.) above the top edges of the side boards, as shown. Nail the boards together.

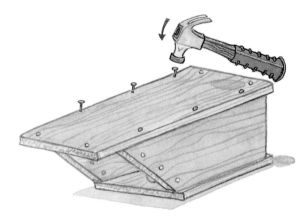

10 Mark and hand drill two $3/32$ in. pilot holes into the sides near the bottom edge, one about 4 cm (1½ in.) from the front on one side and one 4 cm (1½ in.) from the back on the other side.

11 For the bottom, clamp the 14.5 cm (5¾ in.) board and saw 1 cm (½ in.) triangles off the corners for drainage.

12 Insert the bottom into the house so the base is flat. Screw in the screws.

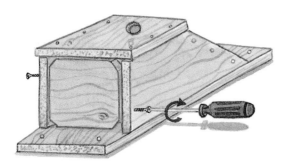

13 For the roof, nail on the 10 x 23 cm (9 in.) board using two 2 in. nails for each side.

14 Using the ¾ in. finishing nails, nail on the molding to cover the gap where the roof and the back board meet.

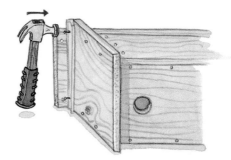

15 To decorate, nail tacks around the hole. (This also keeps predators from gnawing it to make it bigger.) Draw a heart on the front and nail on more tacks. If the wood splits, first drill tiny pilot holes.

Tree house

A hidden hideaway for a nutty nuthatch.

You will need

- pine boards: two 1 x 6 x 28 cm (11 in.),
  1 x 4 x 19 cm (7 ½ in.), 1 x 4 x 27 cm (10 ¾ in.),
  1 x 4 x 10 cm (4 in.), 1 x 8 x 27 cm (10 ¾ in.)
- sixteen 1 ½ in. common nails • two 1 ½ in. screws
- sixty to eighty 1 in. and 1 ½ in. common nails
- about forty 20–30 cm (8–12 in.) long branches,
  1–2 cm (½–¾ in.) thick
- garden pruners • pencil and ruler
- work gloves and safety glasses
- C-clamps, saw, hammer, hand drill with a ³⁄₃₂ in. bit
  and a ¹⁄₁₆ in. bit, power drill and a 1 ¼ in. hole saw
  or spade bit, screwdriver

1 For the front, mark 20 cm (8 in.) on the edge of a long side of one 28 cm (11 in.) board. Using a ruler, draw a line from the mark across to the corner, as shown.

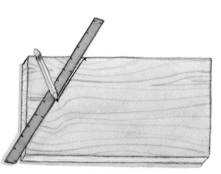

2 Clamp the board to your work surface, and saw along the drawn line.

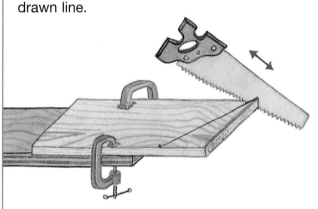

3 For the back, repeat steps 1 and 2 using the other 28 cm (11 in.) board.

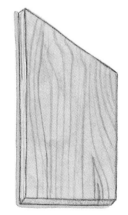
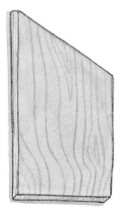

4 On the front board, mark an X in the center, 19 cm (7 ½ in.) up from the bottom edge. Clamp the board and ask an adult to drill a 1¼ in. entrance hole over the X using the power drill.

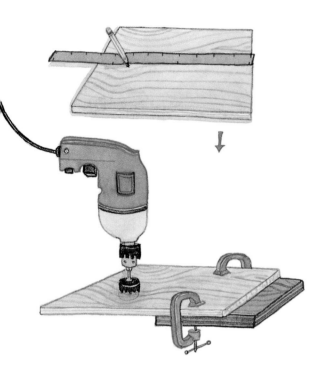

6 Place the front board on the 19 cm (7 ½ in.) and the 4 x 27 cm (10¾ in.) side boards, so the bottom edges are even. Nail the boards together.

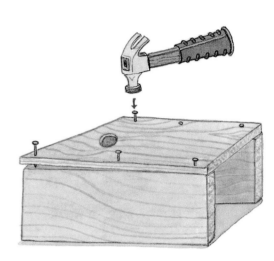

7 Repeat steps 5 and 6 to nail on the back board.

5 Use 1½ in. nails to assemble the house. Hammer three nails into the front board along each side, about 1 cm (½ in.) from the edge, one in the middle and one near each end. The nails should just poke through the other side.

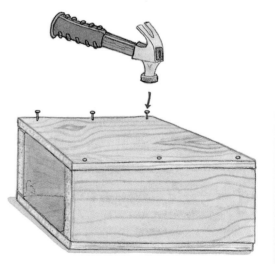

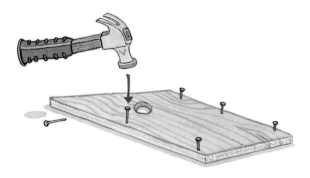

8 For the bottom, clamp the 10 cm (4 in.) board, and saw 1 cm (½ in.) triangles off the corners for drainage.

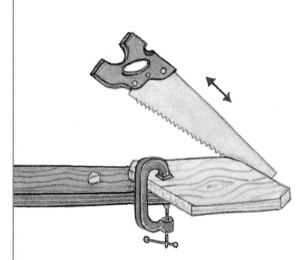

9 Mark and hand drill two ³⁄₃₂ in. pilot holes into the sides near the bottom edges, one about 5 cm (2 in.) from the front on one side and one 5 cm (2 in.) from the back on the other side. Insert the bottom into the house. Screw in the screws.

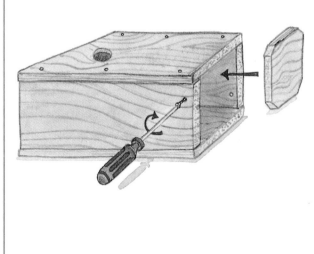

10 For the roof, place the 8 x 27 cm (10 ¾ in.) board on the house so it is even with the back and sticks out about 4 cm (1 ½ in.) past the pointed top. Nail it to the front and back, as shown.

11 To avoid splitting the branches when nailing them to the house, hand drill ¹⁄₁₆ in. pilot holes near the ends.

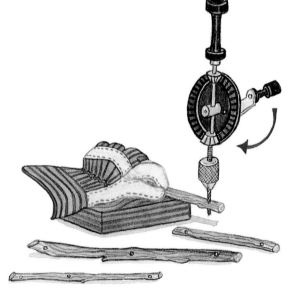

12 Use 1 in. or 1½ in. common nails, depending on the thickness of each branch, to nail the branches to the front, sides and roof, fitting them as tightly together as possible. The nails should not poke through on the inside of the house. Do not cover the screws holding the bottom in place.

13 Nail a few extra branches across the front for decoration.

Other ideas

- Cut some branches to make a pattern.
- Use just a few branches.

Crooked little house

Bluebirds will head straight to this crooked little house.

You will need

- weathered or new pine boards:
  three 1 x 6 x 30 cm (12 in.), 1 x 6 x 18 cm (7 in.),
  1 x 4 x 11 cm (4½ in.), 1 x 8 x 28 cm (11 in.),
  1 x 8 x 14 cm (5½ in.), 1 x 2 x 28 cm (11 in.)
- fourteen #6 1½ in. screws • seven 2 in. common nails
- three 1½ in. common nails • four 1 in. finishing nails
- black upholstery tacks • two wood staples
- wood scraps • 6 cm (2½ in.) length of ¼ in. dowel
- red and black oil pastel crayons and black marker
- pencil, ruler, exterior wood glue
- work gloves and safety glasses
- C-clamps, saw, hammer, hand drill with a ¼ in. bit and
  a ³⁄₃₂ in. bit, power drill and a 1½ in. hole saw,
  screwdriver, sandpaper

1 For the front, mark an X in the center of one 30 cm (12 in.) board, 20 cm (8 in.) from one end.

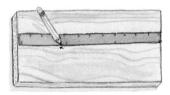

2 Clamp the board to your work surface, and ask an adult to drill a 1½ in. entrance hole over the X using the power drill.

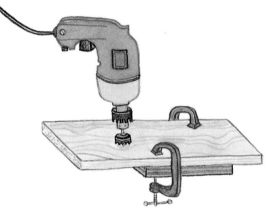

3 On the right edge of the board, make one mark 3 cm (1¼ in.) from the bottom and another mark 9 cm (3½ in.) from the top. Using a ruler, draw lines to join the marks to the opposite corners, as shown.

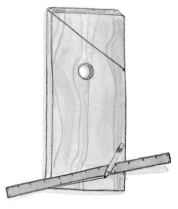

4 Saw off the triangles.

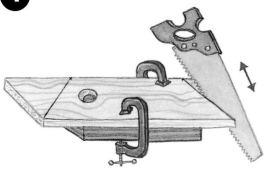

5 Make a mark along the bottom 10 cm (4 in.) from the left edge. Draw a line to join it to the upper right corner, as shown. Saw off the triangle.

6 For the back, place the front piece on another 30 cm (12 in.) board and trace the cut angles. Clamp the back board and saw along the lines.

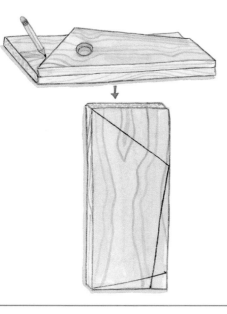

7 For the sides, hand drill three ³⁄₃₂ in. pilot holes about 1 cm (½ in.) from the edge of the 20 cm (8 in.) side of the front board, one in the middle and one near each end. Screw in three screws until they just poke through.

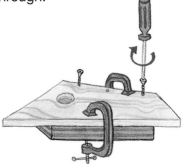

8 Place the front board on the 18 cm (7 in.) board as shown, so the bottom edges are even. Screw the boards together.

9 Hand drill three ³⁄₃₂ in. pilot holes into the third 30 cm (12 in.) board, about 1 cm (½ in.) from the edge, one in the middle and one 5 cm (2 in.) from each end. Screw in three screws until they just poke through the other side.

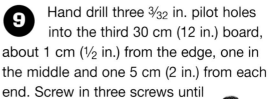

10 Place this board against the front board as shown, so the bottom edges are even. Screw the boards together.

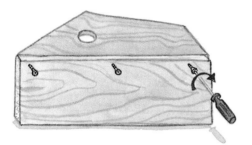

11 Place the back board so the bottom edges are even with the side boards. Hand drill six pilot holes, one in the middle and one near each end of each side. Screw the boards together.

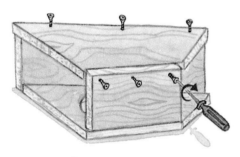

12 For the bottom, clamp the 11 cm (4½ in.) board, and saw 1 cm (½ in.) triangles off the corners for drainage. Fit this board into the house so the base is flat. If necessary, cut the bottom smaller to fit. Screw one screw into each side to hold the bottom in place.

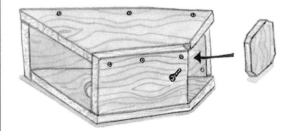

13 For the roof, hammer three 2 in. nails into the 14 cm (5½ in.) roof board about 1 cm (½ in.) from the edge of a long side, as shown. The nails should just poke through the other side.

14 Place the 14 cm (5½ in.) board on the 8 x 28 cm (11 in.) board as shown, and nail them together.

15 Place the roof on the house so that it is even with the back. Nail the longer roof board to the front and back using two 2 in. nails per side.

16 For the chimney, color the 2 x 28 cm (11 in.) board with the marker and pastels to look like bricks. Hand drill a ¼ in. mounting hole 2.5 cm (1 in.) from one end. Using 1 ½ in. nails, nail the board to the back of the house.

18 Cut the door from a scrap of wood. Color it with red pastel and nail it to the front with finishing nails. Press in a tack for the doorknob. Also nail on a doorstep made from a wood scrap.

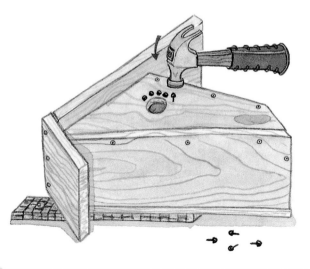

17 Nail tacks around the hole. (This also keeps predators from gnawing it to make it bigger.) If the wood splits, drill small pilot holes first.

19 For the mailbox, round off the top of a 2.5 cm (1 in.) square scrap of wood with sandpaper. Hand drill a ¼ in. hole in the bottom and glue in the dowel. Let dry. Color the mailbox, and use the hammer and staples to attach the post to the house.

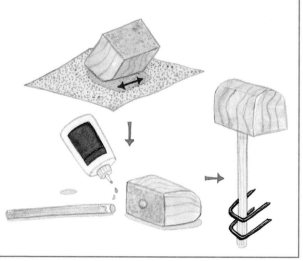

Log cabin

A house sparrow homestead.

You will need

- pine boards: two 1 x 10 x 30 cm (12 in.),
  1 x 10 x 23 cm (9 in.), two 1 x 10 x 29 cm (11½ in.)
- four 2.4 m (8 ft.) lengths of ¾ in. half-round molding
- wood scraps
- eight 1½ in. screws
- nine 2 in. common nails
- four 1 in. common nails
- ¾ in. finishing nails
- pencil, ruler, gray colored pencil
- exterior wood glue and damp rag
- work gloves and safety glasses
- C-clamps, saw, coping saw, hammer, hand drill with a
  ³⁄₃₂ in. bit, power drill with a 1½ in. hole saw,
  screwdriver

1 For the front, mark the middle of the top edge of a 30 cm (12 in.) board. Next, mark 19 cm (7 ½ in.) from the bottom of both sides. Using a ruler, join these marks to the center mark.

2 Clamp the board to your work surface and saw off the triangles.

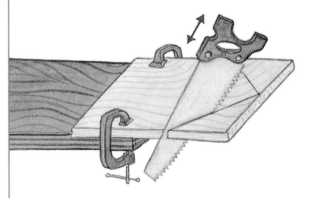

3 For the back, place the front piece on the other 30 cm (12 in.) board and trace the cut angles. Clamp the back board and saw along the lines.

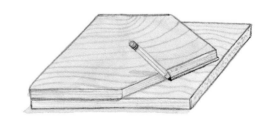

4 For the bottom, clamp the 23 cm (9 in.) board and saw 1 cm (½ in.) triangles off the corners for drainage.

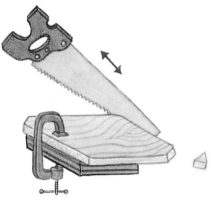

5 Hammer three 2 in. nails into the front board about 1 cm (½ in.) from the bottom edge, one in the middle and one near each end. The nails should just poke through the other side.

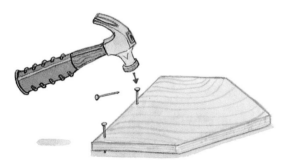

6 Spread glue along one edge of the bottom board. Place the front board on the glued end and nail them together. Wipe off any excess glue.

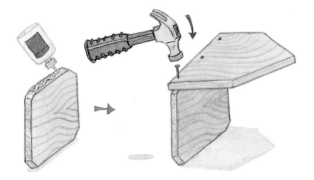

7 Repeat steps 5 and 6 to glue and nail the back to the bottom.

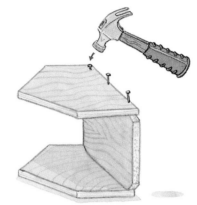

8 Cut eighteen 26.5 cm (10½ in.) lengths of molding with the coping saw.

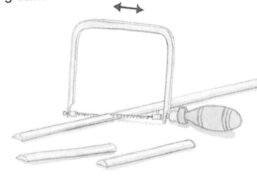

9 Using a finishing nail near each end, nail nine lengths of molding to both sides of the house. Start at the bottom and leave a gap near the edge of the angle for ventilation.

10 Cut a 10 cm x 6 cm (4 in. x 2½ in.) door and a 2.5 cm x 6 cm (1 in. x 2½ in.) doorstep from scrap wood. Glue and nail both to the front with 1 in. nails.

11 Cut a 4 cm x 6 cm (1½ in. x 2½ in.) awning from scrap wood. Spread glue along one long edge and nail it above the door with two finishing nails.

12 For the window, color a small gray square beside the door.

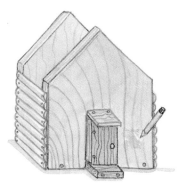

13 For the front, measure and mark each piece of molding you will need, starting at the bottom and working around the door and the window. Saw the molding with the coping saw and nail each piece in place as you go, using a finishing nail near each end.

14 On the front, mark an X in the middle about 17 cm (6¾ in.) from the bottom.

15 Clamp the house, and ask an adult to drill a 1½ in. entrance hole over the X using the power drill.

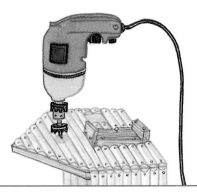

16 For the roof, hammer three 2 in. nails into one 29 cm (11½ in.) roof board along the longer side, as shown, until the nails just poke through the other side.

17 Spread glue on the edge of the other 29 cm (11½ in.) board. Nail the boards together as shown. Wipe off any excess glue.

18 Measure and mark the molding for the front edge of the roof. Cut with the coping saw and nail in place.

19 Place the roof on the house so it is even with the back. Hand drill four ³⁄₃₂ pilot holes about 1 cm (½ in.) from the back edges, then screw the roof to the back using two 1½ in. screws for each side, as shown. Repeat at the front, first measuring how far the roof sticks out.

20 Make a tiny birdhouse from a 2.5 cm x 3.5 cm (1 in. x 1⅜ in.) scrap of wood. Carefully saw off two corners to form the peak. Glue and nail on two ⅛ in. thick scraps for the roof. For the entrance hole, hammer in and then remove a 1 in. nail. Glue the birdhouse to the front of the house.

21 Glue tiny scraps of wood across the window to make the panes.

Space condos

A castle in the sky for purple martins, who love to live together.

You will need

- 15 cm (6 in.) diameter lengths of perforated corrugated plastic drainage pipe: 22 cm (8¾ in.), 33 cm (13 in.), 52 cm (20¾ in.)
- pine board: 1 x 8 x 1 m (40 in.)
- exterior plywood: 45 cm x 45 cm (18 in. x 18 in.)
- twenty-four 1¼ in. round head screws
- twenty-four ¼ in. zinc plate washers
- one 20 cm (8 in.) diameter plastic flowerpot
- two 20 cm (8 in.) diameter plastic funnels
- one small wooden drawer or cabinet knob and a nut to fit
- one black plumbing washer
- eight large colored wooden beads
- four 25 cm (10 in.) dowels narrow enough to fit in the beads
- vinyl electrical tape in a few colors
- one 1 in. plastic plumbing T
- nine 1½ in. flat head screws
- exterior paint and paint brush
- white or yellow colored pencil, pencil, ruler, scissors
- exterior wood glue and damp rag
- work gloves and safety glasses
- C-clamps, coping saw, screwdriver, hand drill with a dowel-sized bit, a ⁷⁄₆₄ in. bit and a ³⁄₁₆ in. bit, power drill with a 2¼ in. hole saw

1 For the first tower, clamp the 22 cm (8¾ in.) pipe to your work surface. Use the white or yellow pencil to make a mark 8.5 cm (3¼ in.) from one end. Ask an adult to drill a 2¼ in. entrance hole over the mark using the power drill.

2 Stand the pipe on the board near one end. Trace the inside of the pipe onto the board with a pencil.

3 Clamp the board and cut out the circle with the coping saw.

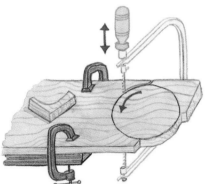

4 Fit the circle into the pipe to make a flat base. Hand drill four $7/64$ in. screw holes around the bottom, through the pipe into the wood.

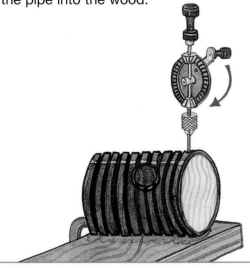

5 Put a washer on each of four $1\frac{1}{4}$ in. round head screws, and screw these into the holes in the base to hold it in place.

6 Hand drill eight $3/16$ in. drainage holes around the pipe, just above the wooden base.

7 Hand drill eight air holes around the pipe about 5 cm (2 in.) from the top edge.

8 Decorate the pipe and the flowerpot roof with electrical tape. Stretch the tape slightly as you stick it on and rub it so it stays on well.

9 For the roof, hand drill a ³⁄₁₆ in. hole in the center of the bottom of the flowerpot. Slide the plumbing washer onto the knob's bolt. Poke the bolt through the hole in the pot and screw on the nut tightly.

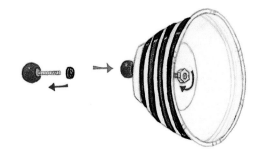

10 Hand drill a hole to fit the dowel on opposite sides of the flowerpot. Place the pot on the pipe and mark the holes. Remove the pot and hand drill holes in the pipe.

11 Put the pot on the pipe and poke a dowel through the holes. Glue a bead on each end of the dowel to hold the roof in place.

12 For the second tower, clamp the 33 cm (13 in.) pipe to your work surface. Mark Xs 8.5 cm (3 ¼ in.) and 24.5 cm (9 ½ in.) from one end. Ask an adult to drill 2 ¼ in. entrance holes over each X using the power drill.

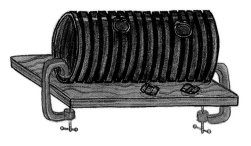

13 Repeat steps 2 and 3 two times to cut out two circles.

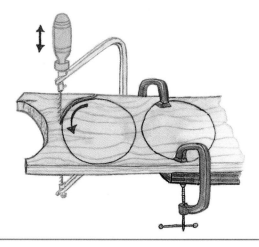

4 Fit a circle into the pipe about 3 cm (1 ¼ in.) below the top hole to make a flat base. Hand drill four ⁷⁄₆₄ in. screw holes through the pipe into the wood. Screw in place as in step 5.

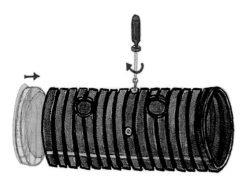

5 With the same pipe, repeat steps 4 to 7.

6 For the roof, glue the plumbing T to one funnel. Decorate the pipe and the funnel with electrical tape.

7 Follow steps 10 and 11 to attach the funnel roof to the pipe.

18 For the third tower, follow steps 12 to 15, adding a third entrance hole 43 cm (17 in.) from the bottom.

19 For the roof, glue a bead to the end of a dowel and let it dry. Poke the other end through the funnel hole from the inside. Glue a bead on just above the funnel tip to seal the hole. Decorate the tip with an electrical tape flag. Follow steps 10 and 11 to attach the roof.

20 Ask an adult to cut a plywood base in the shape you want. One at a time, spread glue on the bottom of each house and screw it to the wooden base using the flat head screws. Paint the base with exterior paint and let it dry.

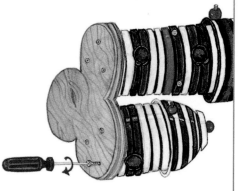

Bird Boot

There was a little chickadee who lived in a boot.

You will need

- an old boot, about 25 cm (10 in.) high
- 10 cm (4 in.) diameter plastic drainage pipe, 20 cm (8 in.) long
- pine boards: 1 x 6 x 20 cm (8 in.), 1 x 8 cm x 8 cm (3 in. x 3 in.)
- four #6 1 in. screws • twelve 1 in. brass nails
- four 1½ in. nails • one black upholstery tack
- two wood staples
- ¼ in. dowel, 6.5 cm (2 ¾ in.) long • wood scraps
- 1.36 L (48 fl. oz.) empty tin can with the ends removed
- oil pastel crayons and permanent black marker
- 10 cm (4 in.) length of 20 gauge galvanized wire
- exterior wood glue and damp rag, 5-minute epoxy
- pencil, ruler, scissors • work gloves and safety glasses
- C-clamps, coping saw, saw, hammer, hand drill with a ¼ in. bit and a ³⁄₃₂ in. bit, power drill with a 1¼ in. hole saw, screwdriver, metal snips, pliers, sandpaper

1 Clamp the pipe to your work surface. Make a mark 15 cm (6 in.) from one end. Ask an adult to drill a 1¼ in. entrance hole over the mark using the power drill.

2 Stand the pipe on the 20 cm (8 in.) board and trace the inside of the pipe onto the board with a pencil. Repeat to draw a second circle.

3 Clamp the board and cut both circles using a coping saw. They should fit into the pipe.

4 Clamp the 8 cm (3 in.) square piece of wood and saw it diagonally across into two triangles.

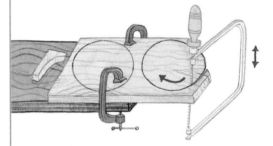

5 Clamp and then hand drill ¼ in. air holes through one circle and the triangles.

6 Spread glue onto the long edge of one triangle and nail it to the circle with two 1½ in. nails, as shown. Repeat with the other triangle on the opposite side of the circle. Wipe off any excess glue.

7 Insert the other circle into the pipe to make a flat base. Hand drill a ³⁄₃₂ in. screw hole on either side through the pipe into the wood. Screw in 1 in. screws.

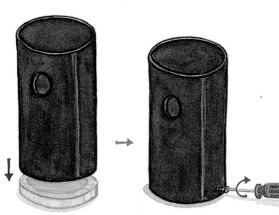

8 Slip the pipe into the boot, base side down. Tie the lace tightly. (Use two laces knotted together to make one very long one.) Feel where the entrance hole in the pipe is, then use scissors to cut out a hole in the boot at the same spot.

9 Insert the top circle into the pipe as shown. hand drill a ³⁄₃₂ in. screw hole on either side of the boot through the pipe. Screw in 1 in. screws to hold the circle in place. (To clean the house, unscrew the screws and remove the circle and roof.)

10 Clamp the boot upside down to your work surface. Hand drill a few ¼ in. holes through the sole and the wooden base for drainage.

11 For the tin roof, carefully cut the can open, wearing work gloves and using the metal snips. Using pliers, bend and flatten the cut ends twice. Bend the roof in half to make a peak that fits over the wooden triangles. Use the brass nails to nail it to the triangles.

12 Roughly color the roof with oil pastel crayons or permanent markers, or leave it to rust naturally. Color the triangles black.

13 Clamp and cut a door from wood scraps with the coping saw. Press in the upholstery tack for the doorknob. Rough up the boot with sandpaper where the door will be attached. Ask an adult to glue on the door using epoxy. Epoxy a scrap of wood below the door for the doorstep.

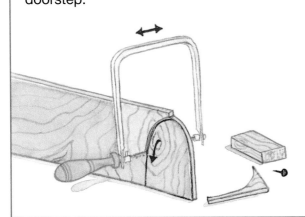

14 To make a mailbox, round off the top of a 2.5 cm (1 in.) square scrap of wood with sandpaper. Drill a small ¼ in. hole in the bottom and glue in the dowel post. Let dry. Color and attach the mailbox post to the sole using the hammer and the wood staples.

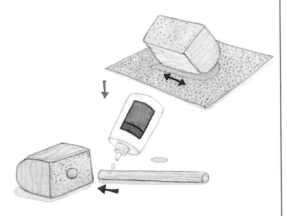

15 Make a sign by hand drilling tiny holes in a scrap of wood. Write the house number in marker on the wood. Slip the wire through a boot eyelet and then through the sign holes. Twist the wire ends together.

Here is more information to change the birdhouse designs to fit other species.

Species	Floor	Wall height	Hole	Where to hang
robins, thrushes, song sparrows, phoebes	15 cm x 15 cm (6 in. x 6 in.)	20 cm (8 in.)	open-sided shelf	almost anywhere
bluebirds, tree warblers, swallows	13 cm x 13 cm (5¼ in. x 5¼ in.)	20–25 cm (8–10 in.)	4 cm (1½ in.)	fences, houses, near open fields
chickadees, nuthatches, downy woodpeckers, brown creepers, titmice	10 cm x 10 cm (4 in. x 4 in.)	20–25 cm (8–10 in.)	3 cm (1¼ in.)	near trees, prefer natural-looking houses
wrens	10 cm x 10 cm (4 in. x 4 in.)	15–20 cm (6–8 in.)	3 cm (1¼ in.)	almost anywhere
house sparrows	25 cm x 25 cm (10 in. x 10 in.)	30 cm+ (12 in.+)	4 cm (1½ in.)	on trees or buildings
purple martins	15 cm x 15 cm (6 in. x 6 in.)	15 cm (6 in.)	5.5 cm (2¼ in.) (3–5 cm [1¼–2 in.] above floor)	nest in groups in open areas
house and purple finches	15 cm x 15 cm (6 in. x 6 in.)	15 cm (6 in.)	5 cm (2 in.)	near woods
screech and saw-whet owls	25 cm x 25 cm (10 in. x 10 in.)	37 cm+ (14½ in.+)	7.5 cm (3 in.)	open fields